Published by Inhabit Media Inc. I www.inhabitmedia.com

Inhabit Media Inc. (Iqaluit) P.O. Box 11125, Iqaluit, Nunavut, X0A 1H0
(Toronto) 191 Eglinton Avenue East, Suite 310, Toronto, Ontario, M4P 1K1

Author photograph by Seporah Medwig
Mamaqtuq Nanook Cooking Club photographs by Kerry McCluskey

Images: Zoeytoja/Shutterstock.com (cover [sprinkles]), Mega Pixel/Shutterstock.com (cover),Seregam/Shutterstock.com (back cover), Svetlana Serebryakova/Shutterstock.com (page ii), Aleksandr Stennikov/Shutterstock.com (page ii), Elenadesign/Shutterstock.com (page iii [paper texture]), azure1/Shutterstock.com (page iii), BoxerX/Shutterstock.com (page iv [polaroid]), Flas100/Shutterstock.com (page iv [paper texture]), Flas100/Shutterstock.com (page iv [paper texture]), Moving Moment/Shutterstock.com (page vi), WitthayaP/Shutterstock.com (page vi), LiliGraphie/Shutterstock.com (page vi), KucherAV/Shutterstock.com (page vi, 4, 6), Miss.Suchada Teeramat/Shutterstock.com (page vi), Danny Smythe/Shutterstock.com (page vi), alexeenko alexey/Shutterstock.com (page viii), arigato/Shutterstock.com (page viii), Leonova Iuliia/Shutterstock.com (page 2), New Africa/Shutterstock.com (page 6), kiboka/Shutterstock.com (page 6), Vladislav Noseek/Shutterstock.com (page 8, 49), rainbow rays/Shutterstock.com (page 9, 21, 22, 32), Mega Pixel/Shutterstock.com (page 10), foto76/Shutterstock.com (page 12), 279photo Studio/Shutterstock.com (page 14), Pixel-Shot/Shutterstock.com (page 14), Amylv/Shutterstock.com (page 14), bigacis/Shutterstock.com (page 14), kiboka/Shutterstock.com (page 16), MaraZe/Shutterstock.com (page 16), Shebeko/Shutterstock.com (page 17), Ira Shpiller/Shutterstock.com (page 17), Viktor1/Shutterstock.com (page 17), Aleksandrs Samuilovs/Shutterstock.com (page 17), Duplass/Shutterstock.com (page 18), Africa Studio/Shutterstock.com (page 18), paintings/Shutterstock.com (page 23), MaraZe/Shutterstock.com (page 23, 28), Seregam/Shutterstock.com (page 25), rodrigobark/Shutterstock.com (page 25), bigacis/Shutterstock.com (page 32), Perepichai Volodymyr/Shutterstock.com (page 32), Cozine/Shutterstock.com (page 32), Robyn Mackenzie/Shutterstock.com (page 35), Bozena Fulawka/Shutterstock.com (page 37), Constantine Pankin/Shutterstock.com (page 47), Anton Starikov/Shutterstock.com (page 48), Alekseykolotvin/Shutterstock.com (page 50), Alp Aksoy/Shutterstock.com (page 51), Jiri Hera/Shutterstock.com (page 51), Suwat wongkham/Shutterstock.com (page 51), bigacis/Shutterstock.com (page 51), AlenKadr/Shutterstock.com (page 56), Wasan Srisawat/Shutterstock.com (page 57)

Editors: Neil Christopher and Grace Shaw
Art Director: Danny Christopher
Designers: Astrid Arijanto and Sam Tse

We acknowledge the support of the Canada Council for the Arts for our publishing program.

This project was made possible in part by the Government of Canada.

Title: Niam! : cooking with kids, inspired by the Mamaqtuq Nanook Cooking Club / by Kerry McCluskey.
Names: McCluskey, Kerry, 1968- author.
Identifiers: Canadiana 20190199369 I ISBN 9781772272550 (hardcover)
Subjects: LCSH: Mamaqtuq Nanook Cooking Club—Juvenile literature. I LCSH: Cooking, Canadian—Nunavut style—Juvenile literature. I LCSH: Cooking—Nunavut—Juvenile literature. I LCGFT: Cookbooks.
Classification: LCC TX652.5 M43 2019 I DDC j641.5/123097195—dc23

Printed in Canada

NIAM!

Cooking with Kids

Inspired by the Mamaqtuq Nanook Cooking Club

by Kerry McCluskey

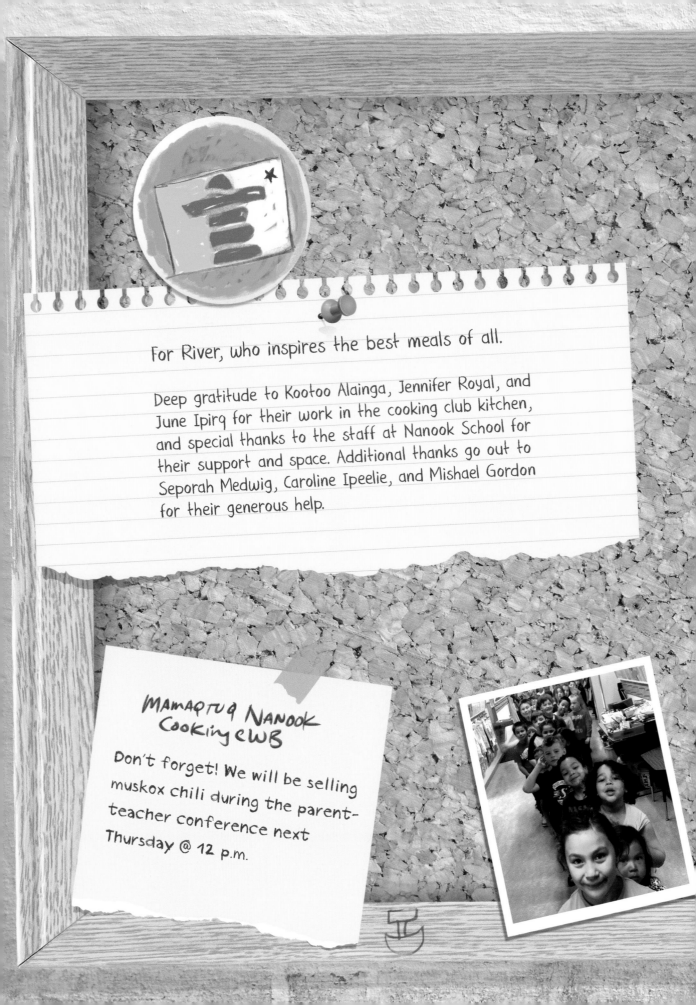

For River, who inspires the best meals of all.

Deep gratitude to Kootoo Alainga, Jennifer Royal, and June Ipirq for their work in the cooking club kitchen, and special thanks to the staff at Nanook School for their support and space. Additional thanks go out to Seporah Medwig, Caroline Ipeelie, and Mishael Gordon for their generous help.

MAMAQTUQ NANOOK
Cooking CWB

Don't forget! We will be selling muskox chili during the parent-teacher conference next Thursday @ 12 p.m.

COOKING CLUB

COOKING CLUB THIS FRIDAY!
3:15 – 5:00pm

NIAM!

CONTENTS

INTRODUCTION

From the time my son could stand, he was on a chair in the kitchen working alongside me, preparing our food. He quickly developed basic cooking skills, which helped build confidence and strong self-esteem. As he got older, he learned to read recipes and write shopping lists, bringing an essential element of literacy development into the kitchen.

Because of our success at home with cooking, I began to look for a way to teach other children basic cooking skills. I found a solution and a welcoming space when my son started to attend kindergarten at Nanook School in Apex, Nunavut. So was born the Mamaqtuq Nanook Cooking Club, a weekly after-school program with the goal of teaching students to prepare healthy food in an enjoyable environment, so they can skillfully feed themselves and eventually their own families. We also focus on literacy development and community volunteerism.

Over the years, I've fine-tuned the program and developed a model that is fun, successful, and transferrable to communities beyond Apex. The recipes included here are simple, kid-tested for fun and tastiness, can be prepared with country foods or store-bought meat, and include ingredients that are readily available in stores in Nunavut communities.

As you work on these recipes in your homes with your children, keep in mind the most important rule we follow at cooking club: have fun!

RECIPE NOTES

These recipes were developed to keep the steps uncomplicated and the ingredients simple. They are basic, flexible, and can easily tolerate substitutions subject to availability of ingredients in Nunavut communities.

Cooks can choose whatever Inuit country food they have access to, including seal, caribou, muskox, moose, or whale meat, or they can choose store-bought meat like beef or pork. For recipes involving poultry, cooks can choose either game birds or chicken, depending on availability. Similarly, for recipes that call for eggs, cooks can use seasonal game eggs or store-bought eggs.

If fresh onions and garlic are unavailable, substitute onion and garlic powder. Many of our recipes use a blended Italian seasoning, but if cooks have access to fresh herbs, feel encouraged to substitute finely chopped fresh herbs. Recipes typically require twice the amount of fresh herbs as dried herbs.

Most of the recipes here will serve a family of four people. At cooking club, we multiply the amount of ingredients several times to make sure there is enough food for everyone.

SAFETY FIRST!

Most of these recipes call for ingredients that are sliced, diced, minced, or grated, which requires the use of a knife or other sharp objects. We recommend using prepared ingredients, like grated cheese or minced garlic, if proper supervision is not available for these steps. Some of the recipes also require working with high temperatures—ingredients need to be sautéed on a stove, for example, or cooked in lard. In order to be safe, these steps also require close adult supervision. It is also important, particularly for the recipes that involve working with meat, to remind children to wash their hands thoroughly before and after handling food. In general, we advise against allowing young children to work alone in the kitchen.

TERMS

Boil: Raise the temperature of a liquid until it bubbles.

Cream: Blend or beat into a creamy mixture.

Dice: Finely chop into small, evenly sized cubes.

Grate: Rub against a sharp surface, like a grater, to break into small or shredded pieces.

Knead: Work flour and water together with your hands to create a smooth ball of dough.

Marinate: Soak or coat with spices and/or liquid before cooking, letting the food absorb the flavour.

Mince: Very finely chop ingredients into tiny pieces.

Purée: Use a hand blender, blender, or food processor to turn fruits or vegetables into a smooth mixture.

Sauté: Fry in oil at a high temperature until ingredients are soft.

Simmer: Cook at a temperature just below a boil.

Whisk: Mix or fluff up quickly, with brisk motions.

ABBREVIATIONS

This cookbook uses common abbreviations for cooking measurements. Beginner cooks might not be familiar with these, so we have included them here for reference.

c: cup   tbsp: tablespoon

tsp: teaspoon   mL: millilitres

SKILLS

The cooking club was created as a way to help teach children how to cook, so we have included a list of skills involved in making each recipe. These skills range from spreading condiments to deep-frying, as we realize that cooks will have varying levels of experience.

COMMUNITY INVOLVEMENT

Mamaqtuq Nanook Cooking Club relies heavily on our community's participation. Whether it is through guest speakers or cooks, organizations opening their doors to us, or donations and other contributions, we would not be as successful as we are without our community lending us a hand. We also endeavour to give back to the community, and teaching our cooks the importance of this is a focal point of our club. Included on pages where the community has been integral to the recipe is a "Community Involvement" box. We use this section to explain the different roles community members play in our club and the ways in which we reciprocate.

Mamaqtuq Nanook
Cooking Club

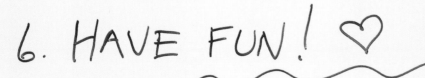

1. Tie your hair back

2. Tie your shoes

3. Keep your hands to yourself
4. Wash your hands with soap and water

5. Listen to Kootoo and Kerry

6. HAVE FUN! ♡

My name is: _____

I like to cook: _____

My favourite food is: _____

I want to learn to cook: _____

COOKING CLUB TIPS

After many years in the cooking club kitchen, we've learned what does and what does not work when cooking with children. On some of the recipe pages, we highlight the lessons we have learned or provide helpful tips on how to use that recipe with your own club.

START YOUR OWN COOKING CLUB

This cookbook is meant to be an educational tool to help teach children the basics of healthy food preparation. It can also be used as a guide to develop a cooking club in another school or community. Following the recipe section in the book, there is a list of steps to follow to help you start and run your own cooking club.

RECIPES

SMOOTHIES

Smoothies are a fun and delicious way to add healthy foods into a child's diet. Kids love picking out ingredients to blend together.

SKILLS

- Choose ingredients
- Measure ingredients
- Use a blender

INGREDIENTS

1 c fresh or 1 ½ c frozen avocado, banana, and baby spinach
1 c water or chilled mint tea
1 tbsp protein powder, plain soy powder, or coconut milk powder

TRY THESE!

Fresh or frozen local berries
Frozen store-bought blueberries,
 raspberries, or strawberries
Frozen mango

Ground flax seed
Watermelon
Peanut butter or soy butter
Soy milk

DIRECTIONS

The best part of a smoothie is that you can make it any flavour you want, but make sure to use equal amounts of fruit and liquid. One cup of fruit makes two servings. Never add more than 1 ½ tablespoons of powders, spreads, or syrups because it will overpower the other wonderful flavours.

1. Blend solid and liquid ingredients together. You may wish to add additional liquid to the mix once blended.

2. Add powder, then blend again.

Community Involvement

Occasionally, parents of children in the cooking club come to teach recipes to our cooks. One parent, Franco Buscemi, and his friend Taha Tabish, provided our cooks with a lesson on smoothie preparation.

Franco and Taha also spoke to the students about the water collection service they provide on Sunday mornings. Annually, they deliver 800 bottles or 15,000 litres of fresh water from Sylvia Grinnell River right to the doors of community elders, keeping up an important Inuit tradition. There's an old saying that this activity is good luck for young Inuit to become good hunters and providers. The service encourages young men to spend time together doing community work, while also connecting regularly with elders.

The service was initiated by the Qanak Collective, an Iqaluit group that was formed to support leadership skills development in the next generation of Inuit leaders and focuses on three priorities: community empowerment, healthy families, and children. Qanak is a project of Tides Canada (www.qanak.com).

SANDWICHES

Sandwiches are an easy way to teach children how to feed themselves healthy food. They are also a great way for kids to experiment and figure out for themselves what they like—as well as which ingredients go well together and which ones do not!

SKILLS

- Choose and assemble ingredients
- Spread condiments
- Slice vegetables

INGREDIENTS

Whole-wheat breads, buns, and/or wraps

Meats (unprocessed if possible)

Dill pickle slices

Hot banana pepper rings

Tomatoes

Cucumbers

Onions

Lettuce

Sliced cheeses

Mayonnaise

Mustard

Nutella

Soy butter

Jams

DIRECTIONS

1. Slice the tomatoes, cucumbers, and onions.

2. Lay out the ingredients and condiments on a table and explain the process. Have kids pick out a type of bread and add their condiment(s) of choice. Then, have them assemble the rest of the sandwich using vegetables, meats, and cheeses according to their personal preferences and imagination. I am always so amazed by their creativity!

MINI QUICHE

Be as creative as you like with
the ingredients you add.

QUICHE

SKILLS

- Measure ingredients
- Use a pastry blender
- Knead dough
- Roll dough
- Crack eggs
- Whisk eggs
- Dice vegetables
- Grate cheese
- Mix ingredients

INGREDIENTS

1 c diced red pepper
½ c diced onion
   or green onion
1 c diced mushroom
1 c diced tomato
1 c grated sharp
   cheddar cheese

12 eggs
1 c milk
1 tsp Italian seasoning
½ tsp salt
½ tsp pepper
12 pastry shells (see recipe on page 21)

DIRECTIONS

1. Preheat the oven to 375°F.

2. Dice the peppers, onions, mushrooms, and tomatoes.

3. Grate the cheese.

4. Crack the eggs into a bowl. It's important when cooking with new cooks to double-check to make sure all shells are removed from the bowl.

5. Whisk the eggs briskly until the whites and the yolks are fully mixed together.

6. Add the milk and whisk briskly again until the milk is fully mixed in.

7. Add vegetables, cheese, Italian seasoning, salt, and pepper, and stir together.

8. Ladle the mixture into pastry shells in muffin tins. Pastry shells should be 2/3 full.

9. Bake for 30 minutes, until the quiche is golden brown and firm.

Community Involvement

We timed the quiche recipe with World Egg Day and brought Iqaluit nutritionist Jayne Murdoch-Flowers in to talk to the kids about how important eating well is to their overall health. This recipe could also be timed with egg-picking season in Nunavut.

PASTRY CRUST

Because our time is limited each week, we use store-bought mini pastry shells for this recipe. If you have the time to make your own pastry, this recipe is excellent and easy. It makes enough pastry for two full-size bottom pie crusts or twelve muffin-tin pie crusts.

INGREDIENTS

½ c butter   ¼ c lard   2 c white flour   ½ c cold water

DIRECTIONS

1. Place the butter and lard into a bowl with the flour.

2. Using a pastry blender, work the ingredients until the mixture resembles a bowl of white peas.

3. Slowly add cold water and mix with a fork until mixture comes together into a ball.

4. Lightly dust a clean surface with flour. Place the dough on the floured surface and gently knead until the ball is smooth.

5. Divide the dough into two portions if using a pie plate, or twelve portions if using a muffin tin.

6. Dust your counter with flour and roll out with a rolling pin and place into pie plate or muffin tin.

Cooking Club Tip

If your cooks are using game eggs in their recipe, bring in a hunter to talk to the kids about how to harvest eggs.

STUFFED POTATO SKINS

SKILLS

- Scoop out potatoes
- Mash potatoes
- Dice vegetables
- Fry and chop bacon
- Measure ingredients
- Mix ingredients

INGREDIENTS

8 large potatoes
1 c diced green onions
1 c cooked, chopped bacon
1 c grated sharp cheddar
  cheese
1 c sour cream

1 tsp garlic powder
1 tsp Italian seasoning
1 tsp paprika
½ tsp salt
½ tsp pepper

DIRECTIONS

1. Preheat oven to 350°F.

2. Wash the potatoes and pierce the skin with a fork in three places to allow steam to escape.

3. Bake for 45 minutes, until the potatoes are soft to the touch.

4. Once the potatoes are completely cooled, slice them in half lengthwise.

5. Using a tablespoon, scoop the inside of the potatoes into a bowl, leaving the skins intact.

6. Mash the potatoes with a potato masher until they are smooth.

7. Dice the green onions.

8. Fry the bacon in a pan on medium heat. Once it is cool enough to touch, chop it into small pieces.

9. Grate the cheese.

10. Add the green onions, bacon, cheese, sour cream, and spices to the mashed potatoes and mix well.

11. Scoop the mixture back into the potato skins, then place the stuffed skins on a baking sheet.

12. Bake for 30 minutes.

PIZZA

Pizza is by far the most popular dish we make at cooking club. Kids love to make it, and they love to eat it.

SKILLS

- Grease pan
- Measure ingredients
- Slice vegetables
- Dice onion and garlic
- Fry and chop bacon
- Cook ground meat
- Mix ingredients
- Sauté
- Purée
- Knead dough
- Roll dough
- Spread sauce

PIZZA DOUGH

INGREDIENTS

4 c very warm water
2 tbsp yeast
½ tsp salt

8-9 c whole wheat or white flour
4 tbsp olive oil

DIRECTIONS

1. Pour warm water into a large bowl.

2. Add the yeast and the salt.

3. Let sit for 15 minutes.

4. When it has stopped bubbling, gradually add the flour, and mix into a ball.

5. Knead the dough for 10 minutes, until the ball is smooth. The dough can be made by hand or in a stand mixer.

6. Generously oil a large bowl.

7. Place the dough ball in the bowl.

8. Cover the bowl with a clean towel and let the dough rise for an hour.

9. Using your fist, punch down the dough to let the air escape.

10. Let the dough rise for another hour. This recipe yields enough dough for four large-sized pizzas.

PIZZA SAUCE

INGREDIENTS

1 large onion or 1 tbsp onion powder
6 cloves garlic or 1 tbsp garlic powder
2 796-ml cans diced tomatoes or 8 fresh,
   large tomatoes
3 tbsp olive oil
2 tbsp Italian seasoning
1 tbsp paprika
1 tsp salt
1 tsp pepper

DIRECTIONS

1. If using fresh ingredients, dice the onion, garlic, and tomatoes. .

2. Add the oil to a large saucepan and sauté the onions until they are golden in colour.

3. Add the garlic and continue to sauté until golden.

4. Add the tomatoes and spices.

5. Cook on low/medium heat for at least 30 minutes.

6. Allow the sauce to cool, then use a hand blender to purée the mixture.

TOPPINGS

Grated mozzarella cheese
Sliced onions
Sliced red or green peppers
Sliced mushrooms
Sliced tomatoes
Pepperoni
Prosciutto
Ground beef, caribou, or muskox
Bacon
Hot banana pepper rings

DIRECTIONS

1. Preheat oven to 450°F.

2. Grease each pizza pan with 1 tablespoon of oil.

3. Sprinkle flour onto a clean work surface.

4. Using a rolling pin, roll the dough into the shape of the pizza pan.

5. Lift the dough onto the pizza pan and spread to the edges.

6. Spread two ladles of pizza sauce onto the dough. Be sure to leave one inch sauce-free at the edge of the pizza.

7. Slice the onions, peppers, mushrooms, and tomatoes.

8. Cook the ground meat in a frying pan until browned.

9. Fry the bacon, then chop into small pieces once it is cool enough to touch.

10. Place the meat, cheese, and toppings of choice on top of the dough, spreading evenly.

11. Bake for about 20 minutes, until the crust is golden brown.

12. Let the pizza cool.

13. Cut into wedges using an *ulu*.

Cooking Club Tip

I always prepare the dough the night before cooking club to save time.
As soon as I finish prepping the dough ball, I place it in a bag and leave it in the fridge overnight. I take it out in the morning and let it come to room temperature during the day, so it is ready to be rolled out at cooking club. I also prepare the sauce the night before.

PALAUGOS

The term "palaugos" is a combination of the words "pogos" and "palaugaaq" (traditional Inuit bannock).
Palaugaaq + pogos = palaugos!

SKILLS

- Measure ingredients
- Mix ingredients
- Roll palaugaaq
- Form palaugaaq dough around sausages/hot dogs
- Deep-fry

INGREDIENTS

8 c flour
1 ¼ tbsp baking powder
1 tsp salt
½ pound lard

3-3 ½ c warm water
Sausages or hot dogs
8 pounds shortening
(for frying palaugos)

DIRECTIONS

1. Mix the dry ingredients together in a large bowl.

2. Add the lard and mix well into the dry ingredients.

3. Make a well in the centre of the mixture and add water.

4. Mix very gently and slowly until you have a thick dough.

5. Let the dough rest for a few minutes.

6. Heat shortening in a large pot.

7. Cut the sausages/hot dogs into halves (optional).

8. Once the dough has rested, take a small ball and stretch it out on a lightly floured surface using your fingers.

9. Place sausage/hot dog on the dough and wrap the dough around it, making sure that the dough sticks. Prepare three or four palaugos before you start adding them to the melted shortening (oil).

10. Test the oil before you start frying by dropping a small piece of dough into the oil. If it rises to the surface, the oil is hot enough.

11. Place palaugos into the oil. As cooking with oil can be dangerous, adult assistance is required for this step.

12. Turn once or twice to ensure even cooking.

13. Remove from the oil once the palaugos are golden brown.

14. Repeat until you have a large batch ready. Be careful! These are very hot.

15. Serve with assorted dips and mustards.

Community Involvement

Qajaaq Ellsworth is a very dedicated parent who frequently comes to cook with us and help us out. Palaugos are one of his specialties: sausage/hot dog wrapped in traditional Inuit palaugaaq, or bannock. The kids go wild for this recipe.

BIRD FINGERS

Bird fingers are a crowd pleaser. I always think of this recipe as one of our most important lessons because our cooks gain a better understanding of how easy and fun it is to cook healthy food they love from scratch instead of buying a box of processed chicken fingers. We focus as much as possible on using whole ingredients and try to avoid processed foods. One of our talented cooks said this recipe was even better than his mother's.

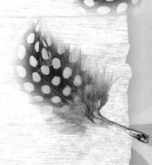

SKILLS

- Measure ingredients
- Crack eggs
- Whisk eggs
- Mix ingredients
- Slice game birds/poultry

INGREDIENTS

4 c boneless, skinless game birds or poultry
4 c 3% milk
4 c white flour
6 eggs
4 c plain bread crumbs
2 tsp Italian seasoning

1 tsp garlic powder
1 tsp paprika
1 tsp salt
1 tsp pepper
1 tsp olive oil

DIRECTIONS

1. Preheat oven to 375°F.

2. Cut the game birds or poultry into strips and set aside in a large bowl. All the pieces should be the same size to ensure equal cooking time.

3. Pour the milk into a bowl.

4. Measure out the flour and put into a separate bowl.

5. Crack the eggs into a separate bowl and beat them.

6. Combine the bread crumbs and spices in a separate bowl.

7. Line your five bowls up in this order: bird fingers, milk, flour, eggs, bread crumbs.

8. Grease a baking sheet with olive oil.

9. Dip the bird fingers into the milk.

10. Remove from the milk and place into the bowl of flour, making sure to thoroughly coat each piece.

11. Remove the bird fingers from the bowl of flour and submerge them in the bowl of eggs.

12. Next, coat them thoroughly in the bread crumb mixture.

13. Place them on the baking sheet.

14. Bake for 30 minutes or until the bird fingers are golden brown and firm to the touch.

JERK CHICKEN

SKILLS

- Use a blender or food processor
- Measure ingredients
- Mix ingredients
- Marinate

INGREDIENTS

3 birds cut into large strips (you'll need more birds with ptarmigan than with goose, duck, or chicken)
1 onion

⅓ c diced green onion
½ tbsp thyme
1 scotch bonnet pepper (for a mild recipe, use ½ a scotch bonnet pepper)

MARINADE

½ tbsp salt
½ tsp garlic powder
1 tbsp pepper
2 tbsp brown sugar

Pinch of paprika
2 tbsp soy sauce
¼ c vinegar

DIRECTIONS

1. Using a blender or food processor, blend the onion, green onion, thyme, and scotch bonnet pepper.

2. Add this mixture to the cut-up birds and coat evenly.

3. Add the dry ingredients for the marinade, making sure the meat is evenly coated.

4. Combine the soy sauce and vinegar, making sure they are mixed well, then pour over the meat. Make sure the meat is well coated and the marinade is evenly distributed.

5. Allow the meat to sit in the marinade for a minimum of half an hour. You can also let it marinate in the fridge overnight. The longer you can soak the meat, the better.

6. Preheat oven to 350°F.

7. Remove the meat from the marinade and place the pieces in a baking dish.

8. Cook for 40 minutes or until the meat is cooked through.

Community Involvement

During Black History Month, Donika Jones from the Nunavut Black History Society came to cooking club and taught us how to make jerk chicken. The kids loved it! Donika served the jerk chicken with delicious Jamaican festival bread.

TACOS

Kids love tacos. They love crunchy shells and they love tortilla wraps. This is a fast and super fun, creative meal to put together and it incorporates all the food groups. Make sure you have plenty of hot sauce and pickled jalapenos on hand because the kids love them. Who doesn't love a good taco party?

SKILLS

- Measure ingredients
- Sauté
- Dice vegetables
- Mince garlic
- Grate cheese
- Fold a tortilla

INGREDIENTS

2 pounds ground meat (tacos are so versatile that any kind of ground meat or poultry is delicious)
3 tbsp olive oil
1 large onion
4 cloves of garlic
½ tsp ground cumin
½ tsp paprika
½ tsp red pepper flakes
½ tsp Italian seasoning
½ tsp salt

½ tsp pepper
4 large tomatoes
2 bunches green onions
4 c grated sharp cheddar cheese
Hard taco shells, large size, and large tortilla shells
2 341-mL cans corn kernels
Pitted black olives
Sour cream
Hot sauce
Pickled jalapeno peppers

DIRECTIONS

1. Dice the onion, place in a pan with olive oil, and sauté until soft.

2. Mince the garlic, add it to the pan with the onion, and continue to sauté.

3. Add meat and spices and sauté until well done. Be sure to drain any residual fat before serving.

4. Dice the tomatoes and green onions.

5. Grate the cheese.

6. Choose a hard taco shell or a tortilla and assemble your tacos!

Cooking Club Tip

We prepare all the ingredients ahead of time and place them out on the prep tables. The kids get to pick and choose what they add. I recommend setting up a few different stations to avoid long lines.

MEATBALLS

SKILLS

- Measure ingredients
- Mix ingredients
- Form meatballs

INGREDIENTS

2 pounds ground meat
  (we recommend caribou
  or muskox)
1 c bread crumbs
1 onion
1 tsp ground cumin

1 tsp Italian seasoning
1 tsp paprika
1 tsp garlic powder
½ tsp salt
½ tsp pepper

DIRECTIONS

1. Dice the onion.

2. Place all of the ingredients in a bowl.

3. Mix thoroughly by hand until all the ingredients are combined.

4. Using a tablespoon, scoop a heaping spoonful of the mixture into your hand and roll into a well-formed ball. You may want to adjust the size of the meatballs you make. We prefer a substantial meatball at cooking club, but others prefer a smaller version. There are many options for cooking.

OPTION 1

This dish can also be prepared in a slow cooker.

1. Bring 8 cups of caribou or beef broth to a boil.

2. Add the meatballs to the broth and reduce heat to medium.

3. Simmer for 45 minutes.

4. Thicken with a flour and water mixture, using two tablespoons of flour mixed with ¼ cup of cold water. Thoroughly shake or blend the mixture to prevent lumps.

5. Stir constantly on low/medium heat for 20 minutes.

6. Serve over rice.

OPTION 2

1. Prepare a pot of tomato sauce using the recipe for pizza sauce on page 26.
2. Once the sauce is hot, place the meatballs in the sauce.
3. Simmer for at least one hour, until sauce is reduced.
4. Serve with your favourite pasta.

OPTION 3

1. Preheat oven to 375°F.
2. Lightly grease a baking sheet.
3. Bake meatballs for 30 minutes.
4. Serve with rice.

Community Involvement

Each year, our cooks hop on a school bus, donated by R. L. Hanson in Iqaluit, and go cook for community members at the Uquutaq Men's Homeless Shelter and the Qayuqtuvik Food Centre. We're very grateful for Hanson's support because it allows us to teach the kids a valuable lesson about caring for their community members that will hopefully stay with them for the rest of their lives.

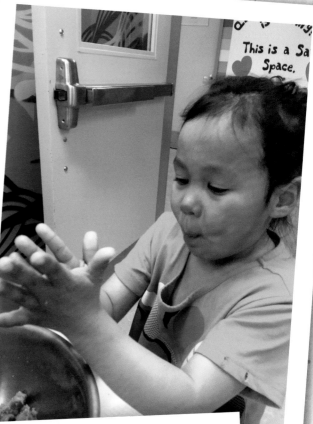

MEATLOVE

Meatlove is another cooking club favourite. We named this recipe in honour of one of our youngest cooks. When she first started cooking club, she was so shy, she didn't speak. She kept her head down, and she was afraid to touch the ingredients or the tools. Within a few weeks, her shyness began to ease away, and her love of cooking began to shine. The day we made meatloaf, she went home and told her *anaana*, her mom, that she learned to make "meatlove" at cooking club. The name stuck.

SKILLS

- Measure ingredients
- Dice onion
- Mince garlic
- Mix ingredients
- Grease muffin tin

INGREDIENTS

2 pounds ground meat
  (we recommend seal
  or muskox)
1 c bread crumbs
1 egg
1 medium onion
4 cloves garlic
Mustard pickles

½ tsp Italian seasoning
½ tsp thyme
½ tsp paprika
½ tsp cumin
½ tsp curry powder
½ tsp salt
½ tsp pepper

DIRECTIONS

1. Preheat oven to 375°F.

2. Dice the onion and mince the garlic.

3. Place all the ingredients into a large bowl and mix until combined.

4. Grease a muffin tin.

5. Place 2/3 c of the mixture into your hands and roll into a ball. Place the meatball into a muffin tin.

6. Repeat step 5 until you have used up all of the mixture.

7. Bake for 30 minutes. Serve with mustard pickles.

Community Involvement

One of our popular guest speakers is Iqaluit resident Joanna Awa, who talked to our cooks about the importance of seals to Inuit:

"The seal is very important to me and to Inuit. The seal was our staple food before Inuit were moved into communities and began the rapid life-changing transformation of government-imposed education and employment in the workforce. Seal was like eggs and bread to us. Other animals were readily available, such as fish, caribou, and whale, but they were seasonal. Seals were always available. Especially during the cold and scarce winter months, the seal was our lifeline. We ate every part of the animal except for the bile sac or the appendix. The skin was used to provide clothing, the fat to burn the *qulliq*

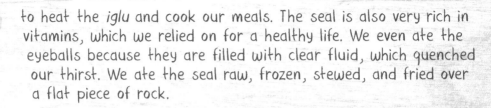

to heat the *iglu* and cook our meals. The seal is also very rich in vitamins, which we relied on for a healthy life. We even ate the eyeballs because they are filled with clear fluid, which quenched our thirst. We ate the seal raw, frozen, stewed, and fried over a flat piece of rock.

Today, in modern times, we can now add dry soup mix, onions, and mustard pickles to our seal meat. We also add other side dishes. But it's so rich that sometimes that's all you need to eat to keep you going for an entire day.

The bones were used to play a game of 'Catch the Animal'
where the little bones were put in a sack with a string that has a
snare. You would put the snare inside the sack and hope you would catch a
piece of bone, so you could say, 'I caught a seal!' Another game we played
with seal bone was 'Will It Happen or Not?'
You would take the shoulder bone and
toss it, but before you do, you would ask
a question like, 'Is our father coming
back from hunting today?' If the bone
landed right side up, your question
was answered favourably, but if it
went sideways, your question was not
answered favourably. The seal ribs
are also perfect when babies were
beginning to eat as they can suck
on the ribs while holding them,
helping them learn how to be more
independent and eat on their own.
The seal is very important to
Inuit and we hope it will always
be part of our regular food."

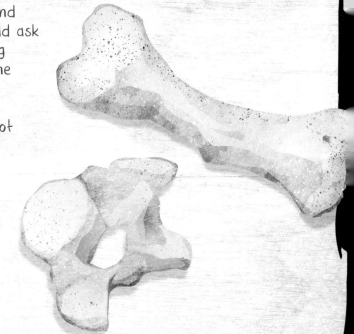

CHILI

Chili can be prepared with any kind of ground meat you have access to, including seal, caribou, muskox, whale, pork, beef, game birds, or poultry. This dish can also be made in the slow cooker. Chili is nutritious and fun because you can work in many different ingredients you have in the fridge.

SKILLS

- Measure ingredients
- Mix ingredients
- Mince garlic
- Sauté
- Dice vegetables

INGREDIENTS

2 pounds ground meat
1 large onion
6 cloves garlic
1 c diced celery
3 tbsp olive oil
2 398-ml cans white or
  red kidney beans, black
  beans, or chickpeas
4 796-ml cans diced
  tomatoes

1 tsp ground cumin
1 tsp paprika
1 tsp chili powder
1 tsp cayenne pepper
1 tsp red pepper flakes
1 tsp coriander seeds
1 tsp Italian seasoning
1 tsp thyme
1 tsp salt
1 tsp pepper

TRY THESE!

2 c diced carrots
2 341-ml cans corn kernels

2 c diced mushrooms
2 c diced red peppers

DIRECTIONS

1. Dice the onion and celery.

2. Mince the garlic.

3. Sauté the onions in the oil in a large saucepan until golden in colour.

4. Add the celery and sauté for a few more minutes until softened.

5. Add the garlic and continue to sauté until the garlic is golden.

6. Add the meat and sauté until well done.

7. Drain any residual fat. This step is best done with the help of a teacher or parent.

8. Add tomatoes, beans, and spices.

9. Stir well and simmer for three hours.

10. Top with sharp cheddar cheese and serve with bread.

Cooking Club Tip

Because chili takes a long time to cook, this is one of those recipes you need to prepare and cook ahead of time, so you have a hot batch of chili to serve the kids after you finish teaching them how to prepare it.

LOVE MUFFINS

SKILLS

- Measure ingredients
- Crack eggs
- Whisk eggs
- Mix ingredients
- Ladle ingredients
- Grease muffin tin

INGREDIENTS

2 c whole-wheat or
  white flour
¼ c brown sugar
3 ½ tsp baking powder
½ tsp salt

1 egg
1 c milk
¼ c melted butter
1 ½ c Nunavut, store-bought,
  or dried berries

DIRECTIONS

1. Preheat oven to 400°F.

2. Grease a muffin tin.

3. Combine the dry ingredients in a bowl.

4. Crack the egg into a separate bowl, beat, and mix with the milk and butter.

5. Add half of the liquid mixture to the dry ingredients and stir with a spoon. Once thoroughly mixed, add the rest and stir again.

6. Add the berries and stir again.

7. Ladle the mixture into the greased muffin tin. Muffin tins should be 2/3 full.

8. Bake for 18 to 20 minutes until golden brown.

Community Involvement

We made these muffins on Valentine's Day. While the muffins were baking, the cooks assembled bags of the dry ingredients and wrote out the recipe to take home to make for their families. They were excited to show off their skills at home.

SUGAR COOKIES

SKILLS

- Measure ingredients
- Crack eggs
- Use electric beaters or a stand mixer
- Line cookie sheet with parchment paper
- Use cookie cutters
- Ice and decorate cookies

INGREDIENTS

2 ¾ c white flour
1 tsp baking soda
½ tsp baking powder
1 c butter, softened

1 ½ c sugar
2 eggs
2 tsp lemon extract

DIRECTIONS

1. Preheat oven to 375°F.

2. Mix the flour, baking soda, and baking powder together.

3. In a separate bowl, use electric beaters or a stand mixer to cream the butter and sugar together until smooth.

4. Beat in the eggs and lemon extract.

5. Blend in the dry ingredients a little at a time.

6. Roll out the dough and cut with cookie cutters. The dough can also be rolled into small balls.

7. Place onto ungreased cookie sheets lined with parchment paper.

8. Bake 8 to 10 minutes, until golden.

9. Decorate with icing, candy, and sprinkles.

Community Involvement

Every fall, cooking club spends weeks preparing for Nanook School's Christmas concert. We bake several types of cookies so when our families and community join us for the concert, we get to showcase our cooking talents for the people we love. This is an important event in cooking club because the positive feedback the kids receive provides them with so much encouragement to keep cooking.

GINGERBREAD COOKIES

SKILLS

- Measure ingredients
- Line cookie sheet with parchment paper
- Crack eggs
- Cream ingredients
- Use electric beaters or a stand mixer
- Ice and decorate cookies

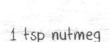

INGREDIENTS

2 ¼ c white flour

2 tbsp minced fresh ginger (or 2 tbsp ground ginger)

1 tsp baking soda

1 tsp cinnamon

1 tsp cloves

1 tsp allspice

1 tsp nutmeg

¼ tsp salt

¾ c butter, softened

1 c white sugar

1 egg

1 tbsp water

¼ c molasses

DIRECTIONS

1. Preheat oven to 350°F.

2. Mix together the flour, ginger, baking soda, cinnamon, cloves, allspice, nutmeg, and salt.

3. In a separate bowl, use electric beaters or a stand mixer to cream together the butter and sugar.

4. Add in the egg, water, and molasses.

5. Stir the dry ingredients into the wet ingredients gradually.

6. Roll out the dough and cut with cookie cutters. The dough can also be formed into small balls.

7. Place onto ungreased cookie sheets lined with parchment paper.

8. Bake for 8 to 10 minutes.

9. Decorate with icing, candy, and sprinkles.

Surprise cookies are a terrific way to use up leftover baking ingredients. This recipe also gives the kids a chance to experiment with ingredients and figure out which textures work together and which do not.

SKILLS

- Measure ingredients
- Mix ingredients
- Balance wet and dry ingredients
- Form cookie dough balls
- Line cookie sheet with parchment paper

INGREDIENTS

1 c rolled oats
1 c raisins
1 c dried cranberries
1 c chocolate chips

1 c shredded coconut
1 c sprinkles
Sweetened condensed milk

DIRECTIONS

1. Measure the dry ingredients into a large bowl.

2. Add enough sweetened condensed milk to make the ingredients stick together.

3. Keep adding dry ingredients and condensed milk until you reach the right consistency. The mixture should be the same consistency as meatballs.

4. Form mixture into small balls and place on an ungreased cookie sheet lined with parchment paper.

5. Freeze until ready to serve.

Cooking Club Tip

We place ingredients at work stations and allow the cooks to pick their own ingredients. We encourage them to roll up their sleeves and get their hands into the bowl. They love it!

START YOUR OWN COOKING CLUB

The key ingredient in a cooking club is a volunteer or volunteers who are committed to organizing and running it. This includes finding the space for the club to meet and cook, finding funding to run the club, and finding the time to plan and execute each week's activity. Listed below is a series of steps to take to help you develop a cooking club in your own community.

Step One: Find a Location

Most Nunavut communities are short on infrastructure, but they all have schools that are equipped with space that can be used to run an after-school cooking club. I approached the school my son attended to ask about developing the program, and the school administration and district education authority were receptive to the idea. Community centres or parish halls may also provide options for space. It is important that the space is donated, because there will likely be no extra funds for rent.

Step Two: Find Funding

I applied for Community Wellness funds from the City of Iqaluit. The Community Wellness funds are administered by the Government of Nunavut. Schools also receive money for breakfast programs and may be able to share their resources with after-school cooking clubs. We also sometimes receive private donations of food and kitchen equipment. Grocery stores may be receptive to providing discounts for cooking clubs, and we have also had success in finding resources through our relationships with other community groups.

Step Three: Develop a Weekly Schedule

If you're like me and are running the cooking club while working a full-time job, it's especially important to be organized to make sure there is time for everything. I plan the week's activity on Tuesday, shop on Wednesday, do prep on Thursday, and run the cooking club on Friday. Altogether, it's a five- to ten-hour weekly commitment. Using the recipes in this book can help you cut down on your planning each week.

Step Four: Running the Club

Choose a day and time when children are available to meet each week. Improvise and turn your school lobby into a makeshift kitchen by setting up tables and work stations. Instruct cooks to tie back their hair, tie their shoelaces, roll up their sleeves, and wash their hands thoroughly with soap and hot water.

Once the cooks are at their stations, explain the recipe to them. Do a significant amount of prep work before the kids arrive at cooking club to make the best use of your time.

Most of the dishes can be prepared and cooked in the time frame allotted, but if the recipe is more complex or requires a longer cooking time, prepare one ahead of time to eat. This is one of the best aspects of cooking club: everyone goes home with a full belly.

Step Five: Make Your Own Cookbooks

While the food cooks, the kids read the recipe and write it down in their cookbooks, contributing to their literacy development. This gets tricky, however, because there is a big difference in the literacy skills of grade one and grade five students. I ask older students to help the younger students until the whole group is done. We also give younger students the easier option of writing down the name of the recipe and drawing a picture of it. We do ask all participants to somehow illustrate each week's recipe because the kids take the cookbooks home at the end of the year and we want to make sure they look nice.

RECIPES

Step Six: Community Volunteerism

Community volunteerism is an important part of cooking club. It makes the program more interesting and provides additional resources. Do research to find out if there are organizations in your community that would benefit from the children coming to cook. Is there a restaurant or a caterer in your community that would allow the kids to tour their kitchen to learn more about food service employment? Field trips teach the kids the importance of helping their fellow community members by volunteering and sharing their time and resources. Bring guest cooks in to share their recipes and cultural knowledge.

Step Seven: Make Use of Media

Mamaqtuq Nanook Cooking Club has been fortunate to receive coverage in northern media, and we have a strong social media presence. We maintain Facebook, Instagram, and Twitter accounts to keep our parents and community informed of our activities. Getting the word out has helped bring in donations of food and other resources to our club. In the initial stages of setting up the club, social media was very helpful in catching the interest of our participants. Be sure to keep your social media sites updated with current information to keep your followers engaged in your activities.

GLOSSARY

For more Inuktitut pronunciation resources, including audio recordings of these terms, please visit inhabitmedia.com/inuitnipingit.

INUKTITUT TERM	PRONUNCIATION	MEANING
anaana	a-NAA-na	mother
iglu	IG-loo	snow house
mamaqtuq	mah-MAQ-toq	tastes good
nanook	na-NUQ	polar bear; most commonly spelled "nanuq"
niam	NI-am	yum or yummy
palaugaaq	pah-LAH-o-gaaq	traditional Inuit bannock
qanak	QAH-nak	tentpole
qulliq	QUL-liq	seal oil lamp
ulu	OO-lu	crescent knife traditionally used by women

Kerry McCluskey is a long-term resident of Iqaluit, Nunavut, and has no plans to return to southern Canada. Kerry and her son, River, like spending time outdoors, at the rink, and in the kitchen.